YOUR AZTEC

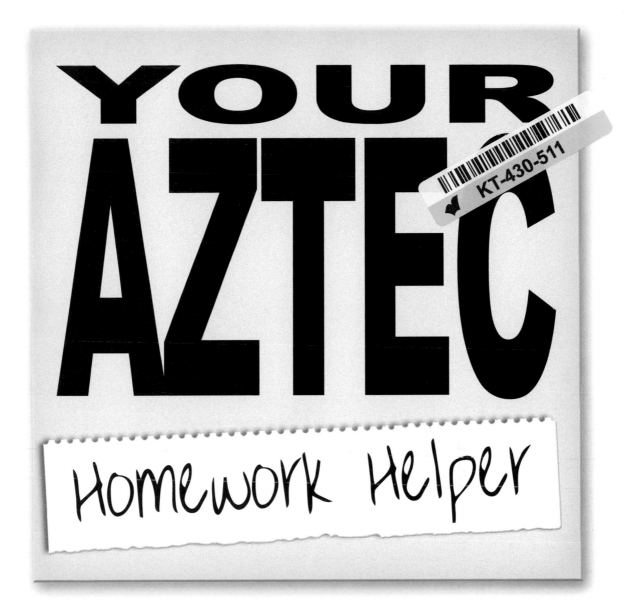

Homework Helper

by Jeremy Smith
Consultant: Dr. Nick Saunders

ticktock
MEDIA

How to use this book

Each topic in this book is clearly labelled and contains all these components:

Topic heading

Introduction to the topic

Sub-topic 1 offers complete information about one aspect of the topic

Choose a word from the Keyword Contents on page 3. Then, turn to the correct page and look for your word in BOLD CAPITALS. This will take you straight to the information you need

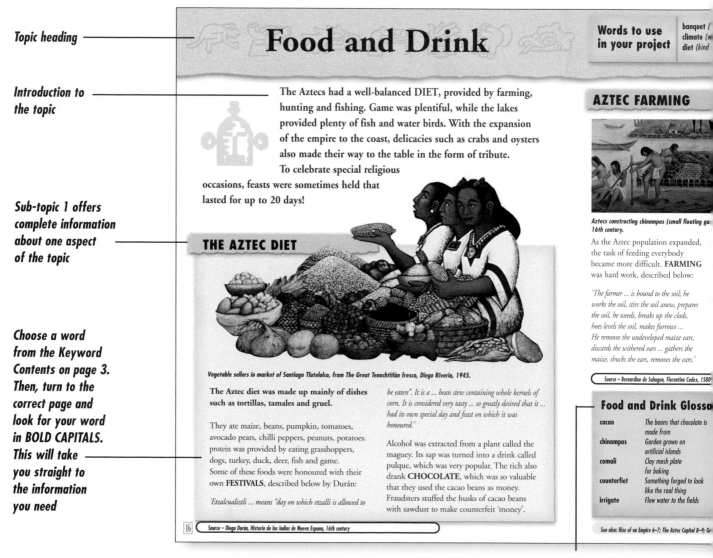

Food and Drink

Words to use in your project
banquet (
climate (w
diet (kind

The Aztecs had a well-balanced DIET, provided by farming, hunting and fishing. Game was plentiful, while the lakes provided plenty of fish and water birds. With the expansion of the empire to the coast, delicacies such as crabs and oysters also made their way to the table in the form of tribute. To celebrate special religious occasions, feasts were sometimes held that lasted for up to 20 days!

AZTEC FARMING

Aztecs constructing chinampas (small floating ga 16th century.

As the Aztec population expanded, the task of feeding everybody became more difficult. **FARMING** was hard work, described below:

'The farmer ... is bound to the soil; he works the soil, stirs the soil anew, prepares the soil, he weeds, breaks up the clods, hoes levels the soil, makes furrows ... He removes the undeveloped maize ears, discards the withered ears ... gathers the maize, shucks the ears, removes the ears.'

Source – Bernardino de Sahagun, Florentine Codex, 1580

THE AZTEC DIET

Vegetable sellers in market of Santiago Tlatelolco, from The Great Tenochtitlán fresco, Diego Riveria, 1945.

The Aztec diet was made up mainly of dishes such as tortillas, tamales and gruel.

They ate maize, beans, pumpkin, tomatoes, avocado pears, chilli peppers, peanuts, potatoes. protein was provided by eating grasshoppers, dogs, turkey, duck, deer, fish and game. Some of these foods were honoured with their own **FESTIVALS**, described below by Durán:

'Etzalcualiztli ... means "day on which etzalli is allowed to be eaten". It is a ... bean stew containing whole kernels of corn. It is considered very tasty ... so greatly desired that it ... had its own special day and feast on which it was honoured.'

Alcohol was extracted from a plant called the maguey. Its sap was turned into a drink called pulque, which was very popular. The rich also drank **CHOCOLATE**, which was so valuable that they used the cacao beans as money. Fraudsters stuffed the husks of cacao beans with sawdust to make counterfeit 'money'.

Source – Diego Durán, Historia de las Indias de Nueva Espana, 16th century

16

Food and Drink Glossa

cacao	The beans that chocolate is made from
chinampas	Garden grown on artificial islands
comali	Clay mesh plate for baking
counterfiet	Something forged to look like the real thing
irrigate	Flow water to the fields

See also: Rise of an Empire 6–7; The Aztec Capital 8–9; Gr

The Glossary explains the meaning of any unusual or difficult words appearing on these two pages

Copyright © *ticktock* Entertainment Ltd 2004
First published in Great Britain in 2004 by *ticktock* Media Ltd.,
Unit 2, Orchard Business Centre, North Farm Road, Tunbridge Wells, Kent, TN2 3XF
We would like to thank: Egan-Reid Ltd for their help with this book.
ISBN 1 86007 541 X HB
ISBN 1 86007 535 5 PB
Printed in China
A CIP catalogue record for this book is available from the British Library.

line (from the gods)
ansion (growth)
vest (process of

gathering in crops)
irrigate *(supply water to*
seafood *(edible fish or shellfish)*

Muro Pico,

luced
lds, irrigation
designed to
. Even swamps
ducing
NDS in lakes
Canoes were
ween fields.
ilies had plots
vegetables
daily diet.

the crops row
nt grows on a cob
holic drink made
aguey sap
at's added to
e something else
ackets filled
savoury filling
avened bread

CASE STUDY

Amazing Maize

Making maize cakes was an Aztec woman's most important task. First, the housewife said a prayer to thank the maize plant for its goodness. Then she would soake the maize in lime water. After this the maize wold be dried and ground into flour. Then she would mix the maize flour with water into a dough, flatten it and cook it on a 'comalli' to make TORTILLAS. At other times, a woman would make the maize into porridge or soup, or she would make 'tamales' (steamed maize-dough envelopes stuffed with savoury fillings). Maize was revered, and great people were compared to the plant. Sahagún describes how one man 'has reached the season of the green maize ear' – meaning he had achieved something very noble.

This polychrome brazier featuring Xilonen, goddess of maize, come from Tlatelolco, Mexico.

Source – Bernardino de Sahagun, Florentine Codex, 1580

17

Keyword Contents

ORIGIN OF THE AZTECS — 4–5
Mexico; capital; empire; valley; volcanoes; lake; city; omen

RISE OF AN EMPIRE — 6–7
power; king; victory; ruled; history; tax

THE AZTEC CAPITAL — 8–9
temples; market; builders; houses; scale; traders

LANGUAGE AND WRITING — 10–11
books; unholy; drawings; carved; scribes; information

AZTEC HOMES — 12–13
buildings; skill; walls; courtyard; mats; rubbish; palace

AZTEC RULERS — 14–15
emperor; changes; bravest; murder; failed; animals; blood offerings

FOOD AND DRINK — 16–17
diet; festivals; chocolate; farming; artificial islands; tortillas

GROWING UP AZTEC — 18–19
schools; boy; girl; symbols; marriage; expectations

AZTEC TIME — 20–21
destroyed; calendars; creation; history; sacred; future

AZTEC SOCIETY — 22–23
nobles; commoners; slaves; peasants; criminals; merchants

RELIGION AND SACRIFICE — 24–25
gods; sacrifice; temple; paradise; skull rack; ritual death

WARS AND WARFARE — 26–27
prisoners; warriors; eagle knights; javelins; priests

LEISURE — 28–29
games; music; gambling; instruments; dancing; poetry

THE END OF THE AZTECS — 30–31
Spaniards; awe; trusting; massacred; hanged; smallpox

INDEX and TIMELINE — 32

Origin of the Aztecs

The most famous civilisation to live in the volcanic highlands of central MEXICO is probably the Aztecs. They arrived on the shores of Lake Texcoco in 1325 AD, and built their CAPITAL Tenochtitlán there. The Aztecs built up a mighty EMPIRE that spread across Central America, yet it had existed for barely three centuries when it was destroyed in 1521 by the Spaniard Hernan Cortés' troops.

A NOMADIC TRIBE

For the early part of their history the group of people known as the 'Mexica' or 'Aztecs' were based in northern Mexico.

According to the friar Diego Durán, who grew up in Mexico City in the 16th century and learned about the Aztecs by interviewing natives, they got their name from the place they lived in:

'The land they inhabited ... was called Aztlán, which means Whiteness or the Place of Herons, and this is why these nations were called Aztec, which signifies "The People of Whiteness".'

Then, between 1100–1200 they left their home in search of more land. Around 1300 they arrived in the Valley of Mexico at the city of Culhuacán. They persuaded the local Culhua king to let them settle there, but in 1323 they were driven out of the city. According to some accounts, this was because the Aztecs had sacrificed the king's favourite daughter after being told to do so by the god Huitzilopochtli.

This illustration shows the long march or migration of the Aztecs to found Tenochtitlan and comes from the Aztec Codex Boturini.

Source — Diego Durán, Historia de las Indias de Nueva España, 16th century

Words to use in your project

culture (customs and beliefs)	
independent	**rules itself**)
nation (country that	**landscape** (countryside)
	mighty (very powerful)
origin (beginning of something)	
settlement (place where a community is set up)	

VALLEY OF MEXICO

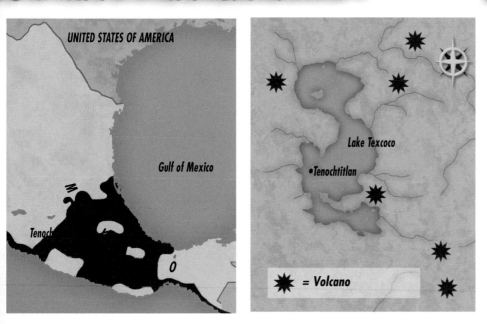

A map of the Valley of Mexico (left) and a close-up of the Aztec Empire (right). The yellow areas show modern-day Mexico, and the red show the extended Aztec Empire in 1519.

The **VALLEY** of Mexico is a large valley surrounded by **VOLCANOES**. In the centre of the valley is the salty Lake Texcoco. The Mexica built their capital on an island in the middle of this **LAKE**. The soil is rich, and it rains a lot during Spring, although for most of the year the land is dry and brown. Around one million Aztecs made their home in the Valley of Mexico, while the highland valleys and plains that surrounded it provided a home for over two million more Aztecs.

Origin of the Aztecs Glossary

civilisation	The way a people live	**Mexica**	Another name for Aztec
empire	Group of states ruled over by one person or state	**migration**	Moving from one area to another
Huitzilopochtli	God of war, and the guardian god of the Aztecs	**omen**	A sign or event that predicts something
legend	A popular story believed to be true history	**tribe**	A group of people with a common culture

See also: Rise of an Empire 6–7; Aztec Time 20–21; Religion and Sacrifice 24–25; The End of the Aztecs 30–31

CASE STUDY

Finding a Home

Aztec legend states that the Aztec people were told where to build a great **CITY** by the god Huitzilopochtli. He appeared in a vision to one of their priests and told him to look for an eagle holding a serpent in its beak, sitting on a cactus on an island in the middle of the lake. Native manuscripts tell us that the **OMEN** came true, and in the early 14th century (1325 AD) the Aztecs settled and began to build their city at a place they named Tenochtitlán or 'Place of the Prickly Pear Cactus'.

'And when the eagle saw the Mexicans, he bowed his head low ... And the god called out to them, he said to them, "O Mexicans, it shall be there!" And then the Mexicans wept, they said, "O happy, O blessed are we! We have beheld the city that shall be ours".'

This illustration from the Florentine Codex shows migration leaders spotting the eagle with a serpent in its beak.

Source – Fernando Alvarado Tezozomoc, *Cronica Mexicayotl*, 1609

Rise of an Empire

When the Aztecs arrived in the Valley of Mexico, they were not the most powerful people there. Two tribes called the Tepanecs and the Acolhua had much greater POWER. At first, the Aztecs worked with the Tepanecs to build an empire. But as they became more powerful, the Aztecs wanted their own leader. In 1372 they made Acamapichtli their 'tlatoani' (KING). Then, at the beginning of the 15th century, led by King Itzcoatl, the Aztecs rose up against their rulers and overthrew them.

THE TRIPLE ALLIANCE

By 1426, hostilities were growing between the Aztecs and the Tepanecs.

War erupted, but in 1428 an alliance between Tenochtitlan, Texcoco, Tlacopan and Huexotzinco defeated the Tepanecs. The Huexotzinca withdrew from fighting but the other three groups drew up an agreement not to attack each other and to group together to conquer other towns. The Codex Chimalpopoca describes the **VICTORY** of the Aztecs:

'In that year 1432, the Tenochtitlán ruler Itzcoatzin (Itzcoatl) was able to come out into the open, for he ruled everywhere, over rulers from town to town.'

This image of fighting at Tlatelolco in Texcoco comes from a manuscript called The Theatre in New Spain, by Panos, 18th century.

Source – Codex Chimalpopoca, 16th century

REWRITING HISTORY

Before the Aztecs, a people called the Toltecs **RULED** over highland central Mexico. In about 1170, the Toltec culture collapsed and Chichimec (the name means 'peoples of the lineage of the dog', or uncivilised people) from the North invaded Mexico. Anxious that his people should not be linked to the lowly Chichimec, Itzcoatl ordered the traditional **HISTORY** books to be burnt and new history books to be written. This showed how the Mexica were the special people of the god Huitzilopochtli, and that their rulers were descended from the civilised Toltec kings:

'It is not wise that all the people should know the paintings. The common people would be driven to ruin and there would be trouble, because these paintings contain many lies. For many in the pictures have been hailed as gods.'

Stone statue of warrior from the Toltec city of Tula.

Source – Bernardino de Sahagún, Códice Matritense de la Real Academia, 16th century

Rise of an Empire Glossary

alliance	A union to pursue common interests		by force
		territory	Area controlled by ruler or state
descended	Family relative of		
empire	Group of states ruled over by one person or state	**tlatoani**	An Aztec king or emperor
		tribute	Payment by conquered people to another, more powerful, nation
hostilities	Difficulties and tensions		
overthrew	Removed from power		

CASE STUDY

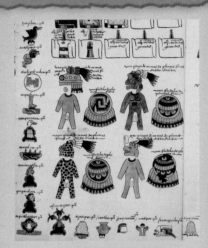

Tribute from 16 towns, including women's tunics and skirts, and warrior costumes and shields. Taken from the Codex Mendoza, probably written early 1540s.

Paying Tribute

As the 15th century progressed, the Aztec empire got larger and larger. When a territory was captured, the conquered people were usually allowed to rule themselves, but they were made to pay an annual **TAX** called a 'tribute' to the Aztec Emperor. As a result, a staggering amount of riches flowed into the capital Tenochtitlan. The friar Diego Durán described the sort of goods the people of the empire were made to give as payment:

'The subjects of the lords of Tenochtitlan paid all kinds of tribute – food, clothing weapons ... The poorest among them, lacking what was necessary, offered their sons and daughters.'

Source – Diego Durán, The History of the Indies of New Spain, 1581

See also: Origin of the Aztecs 4–5; The Aztec Capital 8–9; Language and Writing 10–11; Aztec Rulers 14–15

The Aztec Capital

The Aztec capital of Tenochtitlán lies underneath the streets of modern Mexico City. Bits of the Aztec city often emerge when building work takes place in the Mexican capital. TEMPLES, sacrificial platforms and statues of gods have all been discovered in recent years. At its height, Tenochtitlan would have been a busy place, dominated by the Great Temple and the MARKET at Tlatelolco, just outside the city.

THE FOUNDING OF TENOCHTITLÁN

This map of Tenochtitlán is attributed to Hernán Cortés.

Despite the fact that the site chosen for Tenochtitlán was on swampland, the Aztec BUILDERS conquered the difficult terrain.

The friar Diego Durán recorded the skill in which this was done by interviewing natives:

'Little by little they ... created space for their city; on top of the water they made a foundation with earth and stones that were thrown into the spaces between the stakes, in order to lay out their city on that surface.'

The Codex Mendoza's opening page shows that the city was divided into four quarters. By measuring the orientations of buildings, and examining 16th-century Spanish maps, archaeologists have shown that Tenochtitlán was built on a grid plan that was aligned to the gods. The east-west line was considered the most important because it tracked the path of the sun god Tonatiuh across the sky.

Source – Diego Durán, Historia de las Indias de Nueva Espana, 16th century

SPANISH IMPRESSIONS

Descriptions of the city of Tenochtitlán were recorded by Cortés himself in letters written to the King of Spain.

16th-century portrait of the Spanish leader Cortés.

Cortés reported that it had 60,000 **HOUSES** and covered an area of five square miles.

'The city is so big and so remarkable ... with as good buildings and many more people than Granada had when it was taken.'(1)

The Spanish foot soldier Bernal Díaz del Castillo was also stunned by the **SCALE** of the city.

'When we saw all those cities and villages built in the water, and that straight and level causeway leading to the city, we were astounded. It all seemed so like a vision from a fantasy story that some of our soldiers asked if it was a dream. It was so wonderful that I do not know how to describe the first sight of things never seen, or heard of, or dreamed of before.'(2)

Source – Hernán Cortés, Letters from Mexico, 16th century (1) and Bernal Diaz, The Conquest of New Spain, 16th century (2)

The Aztec Capital Glossary

aligned	Placed in a straight line		are parallel to each other with others at right angles
archaeologists	People who study history by digging up objects	**orientation**	Angle
causeway	A raised road built to get across water	**scale**	Size
		swampland	Area of waterlogged ground
grid plan	Laid out so that roads	**terrain**	Land

CASE STUDY

This mural by D. Hernandez Xochitiotzin of a market in Tlaxcala shows daily life before the Spanish conquest.

The Great Market

Aztecs flocked to a great market at Tlatelolco, just outside Tenochtitlan. The Spanish priest Sahagún tells us that up to 60,000 people went to market every day, and that 'given the choice between going to market and going to heaven, the normal Aztec housewife chose heaven, but asked if she could go to the market first!' His writings in the Florentine Codex also give us a glimpse of how **TRADERS** bought and sold there:

'The ruler took care of the directing of the marketplace and all things sold, for the good of the common folk ... so that these might not be abused, not suffer harm, not be deceived, not disdained .... Marketplace directors were appointed to office. Each of the directors took care, and was charged, that no one might deceive another, and how (articles) might be priced and sold.'

Source – Bernardino de Sahagún, Florentine Codex, c. 16th century

See also: Origin of the Aztecs 4–5; Rise of an Empire 6–7; Aztec Homes 12–13; The End of the Aztecs 30–31

Language and Writing

The Aztecs recorded their history using a picture-based language called 'pictographs'. Scribes drew the pictographs in special BOOKS called 'codices'. When the Spanish took control of Mexico in 1519, the new Christian rulers burnt any books they could find, viewing them as UNHOLY. Only one pre-conquest example of Aztec writing survives. The other examples of the Aztec language we have are codices drawn up after the conquest.

AZTEC CODICES

The Aztecs used pictures, or glyphs, for their writing system, just as the Chinese and Japanese do today.

Some glyphs were **DRAWINGS** of the objects themselves and some were meant to show ideas. A shield and a club, for example, meant war. Aztec glyphs were **CARVED** on objects such as stone monuments and tiny jade beads, painted on walls and vases, and painted in books made of bark called 'codices'. Many glyphs were calendar and numeric signs, but some represented historic events. An example of this is in the Codex Mendoza, which documents the Aztec army conquering other cities. To show that a city has been conquered, the city's name is written next to the 'conquered' glyph which is a temple (pyramid) in smoke and flames with the top part toppling over.

Illustrations from the Codex Mendoza showing the glyph 'burning-temple' representing a conquered city.

Words to use in your project

account *(story)*
bias *(distortion of the facts)*
dialect *(form of language used*

by a particular group)
ritual *(actions involved with religious ceremony)*

sources *(documents providing evidence)*
traditional *(local custom)*

WRITTEN RECORDS

Aztec books had no covers but were protected by a wooden board at each end when they were folded up.

Running the Aztec empire meant that **SCRIBES** were busy people. They had to record who had paid taxes, while merchants kept records of accounts, and temples owned libraries of religious works. One Aztec ruler describes just how many scribes there were in Aztec society:

'They had scribes for each branch of knowledge. Some dealt with the annals, putting down in order the things which happened each year, giving the day,

month, and hour. Others ... recorded the lineage of rulers, lords and noblemen, registering the newborn and deleting those who had died. The priests recorded all matters to do with the temples and images ... and finally, the philosophers and learned men which there were among them were charged with painting all the sciences which they had discovered, and with teaching by memory all the songs in which were embodied their scientific knowledge and historical traditions.'

Source – Fernando de Avala Ixtlilxochitl, Historia Tolteca-Chichimeca, c. 1550

Language and Writing Glossary

annals	*Historical record*	**glyph**	*A picture symbol for a word or phrase*
codices	*(singular: codex) Books made by folding pages made of bark*	**Nahuatl**	*The Aztec language*
		scribes	*People whose job is to write things*
embodied	*Included as part of*		

See also: The Aztec Capital 8–9; Growing Up Aztec 18–19; Aztec Society: 22–23; The End of the Aztecs 30–31

CASE STUDY

The Codex Florentine and the Codex Mendoza

The Codex Florentine was compiled by Friar Bernardino de Sahagún between 1577 and 1580. He spoke with old men and told them to paint their stories in the traditional Mexica way. The native text, Nahuatl, appears in the right column, with Spanish text in the left column. The Codex provides a rich source of **INFORMATION** for the Aztec view of life. There is information on health, lifestyles, rituals, attitudes towards law and order and drunkenness, and even a few Aztec jokes!

The Codex Mendoza was prepared for King Charles V of Spain. It was written using the native pictographic system of writing, with explanations of what was going on written in the margins by a Spanish priest. It tells us about customs, rites and everyday life, and also all about the many signs or glyphs that were used to represent place names and titles of warriors, for example.

Illustration from Codex Mendoza showing tribute list paid by a city, including precious greenstones and clothing.

Source – Ixtlilxochitl, Historia Chichimeca

Remains of Aztec BUILDINGS and paintings in the codices help us to learn a lot about how the Aztecs lived. The houses of rich Aztecs were big and flat-roofed, and had two storeys. Peasant houses were a lot smaller and were often built in groups. The soldier Diaz, who travelled to Mexico with Cortés' army, observed that his lodging had been prepared with such SKILL 'that one of the horsemen took the shining whiteness for silver, and came galloping back to tell Cortés that our quarters had silver walls.'

RICH AND POOR

The remains of Aztec peasants' houses show that, although some had stone WALLS, most had mud-brick walls and thatched roofs made from maguey leaves.

Peasant houses were often built in a group (called a 'cemithualtin') of five or six buildings grouped around a COURTYARD. Often the houses were so tiny that everything – cooking, washing, working and relaxing – must have taken place outside in this courtyard.

Wealthy citizens lived in bigger houses hidden behind windowless walls. Inside, the rooms opened out onto a central courtyard, often with a pond and gardens of brightly coloured flowers. Inside, everybody slept on MATS, as noted by Bernal Díaz:

'However great a lord he might be, no one had any bed other than this kind.'

This illustration of The House of Rain comes from the Aztec Codex Vaticanus, 16th century.

Source – Bernal Díaz de Castillo, The Conquest of New Spain, 16th century

HOUSING

Ruins at the villages of Capilco and Cuexcomate give us an idea of what life might have been like in the Aztec countryside. The small farming hamlet of Capilco had 21 houses, while Cuexcomate had 150. Houses were tiny, and people probably spent most of their time on the patio outside. Archaeologists have found hundreds of objects at the side of houses, suggesting that people threw their **RUBBISH** there. The Friar Sahagún records something that supports this theory:

'Aztec babies spend their time piling up earth and potsherds, those on the ground.'

In late Aztec times it seems that the population was growing – as excavations have uncovered evidence of an increase in dam-building to irrigate more land and produce more food.

Ruins of the Aztec settlement at Cuexcomate.

Source – Friar Bernardino de Sahagún, Florentine Codex: General History of the Things of New Spain, 16th century

Aztec Homes Glossary

cemithualtin	*A Nahuatl word meaning a group of peasant houses*		*mud and straw*
excavated	*Things dug up for studying history*	**maguey**	*A plant used for brewing alcohol, making roofs and plaiting into threads*
irrigate	*Supply water by channels*	**lodging**	*Temporary home*
mud-brick	*Bricks made from dried*	**potsherds**	*Pieces of broken pottery*

CASE STUDY

Part of the ruined palace at Yautepec, Mexico.

An Aztec Palace

In 1989, at the modern town of Yautepec in Mexico, archaeologists discovered an enormous stone platform of more than half a hectare. It had been the site of the **PALACE** of the powerful tlatoani of Yautepec. They discovered that the stone palace walls had been four metres high, and that there was just one entrance, at the top of a single stairway. On the platform were many courtyards, rooms and passages, all constructed of stone covered with layers of lime plaster and decorated with colourful paintings. It was the first Aztec royal palace to be excavated. On the outside, a plain stone wall kept the public out. Inside, the buildings faced onto a central courtyard.

See also: Origin of the Aztecs 4–5; The Aztec Capital 8–9; Food and Drink 16–17; Aztec Society 22–23

Aztec Rulers

In 1372, Acamapichtli became the first Aztec tlatoani, or EMPEROR. He was succeeded by Huitzilihuitl, under whom the city of Tenochtitlán grew. Under the rule of the fourth emperor, Itzcoatl, the Aztecs defeated their neighbours and built a powerful empire, upon which future emperors would build.

AZTEC RULERS

Acamapichtli *(1372–1391)*
Huitzilihuitl *(1391–1415)*
Chimalpopoca *(1415–1426)*
Itzcoatl *(1426–1440)*
Moctezuma I *(1440–1468)*
Axayacatl *(1468–1481)*
Tizoc *(1481–1486)*
Ahuitzotl *(1486–1502)*
Moctezuma II *(1502–1520)*
Cuitlahuac *(1520)*
Cuauhtemoc *(1520–1525)*

MOCTEZUMA I

The Emperor Moctezuma I succeeded Itzcoatl in 1440. Building on the success of his predecessor, Moctezuma expanded the Aztec empire.

He expanded Aztec territory by invading tropical areas of Mexico, including the city of Coixtlahuaca in 1458. Moctezuma also introduced a number of **CHANGES** to Aztec society. The Spanish friar Diego Durán tells us how he introduced a series of new laws that made the distinction between nobles and commoners even greater:

- *Only the king and the prime minister ... may wear sandals within the palace.*
- *The commoners will not be allowed to wear cotton clothing, under pain of death, but can only use garments of maguey fiber.*
- *Only the great noblemen and valiant warriors are given licence to build a house with a second storey; for disobeying this law a person receives the death penalty.*
- *Thieves will be sold for the price of their theft, unless the theft be grave, having been committed many times. Such thieves will be punished by death.'*

Moctezuma also allowed some commoners to gain influence through their own talents. He created a new position called Quauhpilli – Eagle Lord. It was awarded to the **BRAVEST** soldiers in his army.

This illustration of Moctezuma I comes from the Codex Mendoza.

Source – Diego Durán, Historia de las Indias de Nueva Espana, 16th century

MOCTEZUMA II

From the 1470s, the Aztec empire suffered a series of setbacks, ending in the **MURDER** of the emperor Tizoc in 1486. His brother Ahuitzotl then ruled for 16 years before Moctezuma II succeeded as emperor in 1502. The new emperor removed many officials that had served under his predecessor, Ahuitzotl. Under the new emperor, the empire swelled, but **FAILED** to defeat the Aztec's powerful neighbours, the Tlaxcala. Moctezuma was fearful about the future. Nezahualpilli, a past king of Texcoco earlier, appeared to him in a dream, according to Diego Durán:

'Nezahualpilli spoke to Moctezuma in a dream as follows, showing him the future portents. "I must inform you of strange and marvellous things which must come about during your reign".'

Moctezuma (1466–1520), emperor of the Aztecs, 16th century detail.

Source – Diego Durán, *Historia de las Indias de Nueva España*, 16th century

Aztec Rulers Glossary

commoners	Ordinary people		Eagle lords
coronation	Ceremony of crowning a new king or queen	portents	Sign that something bad is going to happen
predecessor	Person who held job before current holder	reign	Rule (like a king or queen)
		seclusion	Being alone
Quauhpilli	A Nahuatl word meaning	succeeded	Came after

See also: Rise of an Empire 6–7; Aztec Homes 12–13; Wars and Warfare 26–27; The End of the Aztecs 30–31

CASE STUDY

Coronation of Moctezuma II, from the *Historia de los Indios* by Diego Durán, 1579.

The Power of the Emperor

Diego Durán's *Historia de los Indios* gives us an understanding of the power an emperor had in Aztec society. It shows rulers seated on thrones covered with the skins of powerful **ANIMALS**, such as the jaguar. This codex also records the coronation of emperors during which they prayed to their patron god Tezcatlipoca for guidance. Also shown is the final ceremony of the imperial coronation involving a period of seclusion and **BLOOD OFFERINGS**.

Food and Drink

The Aztecs had a well-balanced DIET, provided by farming, hunting and fishing. Game was plentiful, while the lakes provided plenty of fish and water birds. As the empire grew towards the coast, delicacies such as crabs and oysters also made their way to the table. To celebrate special religious occasions, feasts were sometimes held that lasted for up to 20 days!

THE AZTEC DIET

Vegetable sellers in market of Santiago Tlatelolco, from The Great Tenochtitlán fresco, Diego Riveria, 1945.

The Aztec diet included dishes such as tortillas, tamales and gruel.

They ate maize, beans, pumpkin, tomatoes, avocado pears, chilli peppers, peanuts, potatoes. Protein was provided by eating grasshoppers, dogs, turkey, duck, deer, fish and game. Some of these foods were honoured with their own **FESTIVALS**, as described by Durán:

'*Etzalcualiztli ... means "day on which etzalli is allowed to be eaten". It is a ... bean stew containing whole kernels of corn. It is considered very tasty ... so greatly desired that it ... had its own special day and feast on which it was honoured.*'

Alcohol was extracted from a plant called the maguey. Its sap was turned into a drink called pulque, which was very popular. The rich also drank **CHOCOLATE**, which was so valuable that they used the cacao beans as money. Criminals stuffed the husks of cacao beans with sawdust to make counterfeit 'money'.

Source – Diego Durán, Historia de las Indias de Nueva Espana, 16th century

Words to use in your project

banquet *(feast)*
climate *(weather)*
diet *(kind of food a person eats)*

divine *(from the gods)*
expansion *(growth)*
harvest *(process of*

gathering in crops)*
irrigate *(supply water to*
seafood *(edible fish or shellfish)*

AZTEC FARMING

Aztecs constructing chinampas (small floating gardens on reed rafts), by Jose Muro Pico, 16th century.

As the Aztec population expanded, the task of feeding everybody became more difficult. **FARMING** was hard work, described below:

'The farmer ... is bound to the soil; he works the soil, stirs the soil anew, prepares the soil, he weeds, breaks up the clods, hoes level the soil, makes furrows ... He removes the undeveloped maize ears, discards the withered ears ... gathers the maize, shucks the ears, removes the ears.'

Aztec farmers introduced terracing in their fields, irrigation and other methods designed to produce more crops. Even swamps were farmed by producing **ARTIFICIAL ISLANDS** in lakes called 'chinampas'. Canoes were used for moving between fields. In towns, most families had plots of land for growing vegetables to supplement their daily diet.

Source – Bernardino de Sahagún, Florentine Codex, 1580

Food and Drink Glossary

cacao	The beans that chocolate is made from		to help the crops grow
chinampas	Gardens grown on artificial islands	maize	Grain that grows on a cob
comalli	Clay mesh plate for baking	pulque	An alcoholic drink made from maguey sap
counterfeit	Something forged to look like the real thing	supplement	Thing that's added to improve something else
irrigate	Flow water to the fields	tamales	Maize packets filled with a savoury filling
		tortillas	An unleavend bread

See also: Rise of an Empire 6–7; The Aztec Capital 8–9; Growing Up Aztec 18–19

CASE STUDY

Amazing Maize

Making maize cakes was an Aztec woman's most important task. First, the woman would say a prayer to thank the maize plant for its goodness. Then she would soak the maize in lime water. After this the maize would be dried and ground into flour. Then she would mix the maize flour with water into a dough, flatten it and cook it on a 'comalli' to make **TORTILLAS**. At other times, a woman would make the maize into porridge or soup, or she would make 'tamales' (steamed maize-dough envelopes stuffed with savoury fillings). Maize was revered, and great people were compared to the plant. Sahagún describes how one man 'has reached the season of the green maize ear' – meaning he had achieved something very noble.

This polychrome brazier featuring Xilonen the goddess of maize, came from Tlatelolco, Mexico.

Source – Bernardino de Sahagún, Florentine Codex, 1580

Growing Up Aztec

Aztec boys began school at 15. Commoners went to SCHOOLS called 'telpochcalli'. Students learned manual skills, how to sing and dance, and military training which was taught by experienced warriors. Noble children went to more exclusive schools known as 'calmecac'. Associated with temples, their aim was to educate the next generation of leaders in government, the priesthood and the army. Girls did not go to school at all.

EDUCATION

The Codex Mendoza tells us much about education for Aztec children.

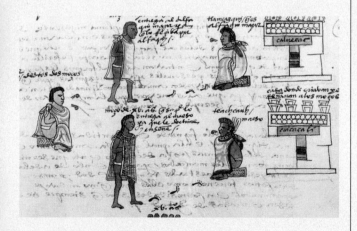

BOYS

For a **BOY**, there were two routes of further education. The father, seated on the left, could send his son to the head priest for training at the temple school (calmecac) for noble boys. Alternatively (below) he could give his son to the master of youths at 'the young men's house' (telpochcalli), where military training was provided for commoners.

GIRLS

When a **GIRL** reached the age of 15, she was ready to get married. At the bottom of this picture, a torch-lit procession accompanies the bride to the groom's house on the first night. Inside, a feast is laid out. Four elderly wedding guests are shown talking. The bride and her older groom, their garments tied together, sit in front of a hearth and a bowl of incense, on the mat on which they will eventually sleep.

Source – Codex Mendoza, 14th century

Words to use in your project

breadwinner *(person who earns money to support family)*
composure *(self-control)*

instruction *(education)*
military *(related to war)*
nurture *(to raise something)*

occupation *(job or profession)*
upbringing *(treatment from parents during childhood)*

MARRIED LIFE

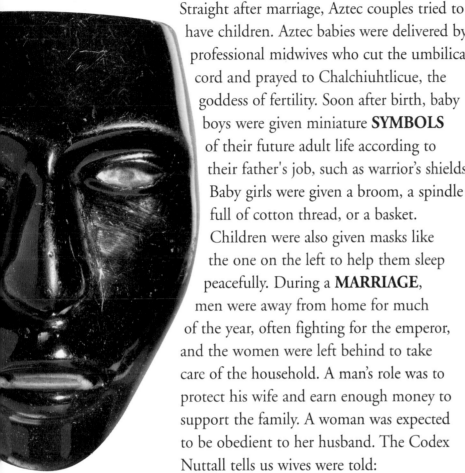

Straight after marriage, Aztec couples tried to have children. Aztec babies were delivered by professional midwives who cut the umbilical cord and prayed to Chalchiuhtlicue, the goddess of fertility. Soon after birth, baby boys were given miniature **SYMBOLS** of their future adult life according to their father's job, such as warrior's shields. Baby girls were given a broom, a spindle full of cotton thread, or a basket. Children were also given masks like the one on the left to help them sleep peacefully. During a **MARRIAGE**, men were away from home for much of the year, often fighting for the emperor, and the women were left behind to take care of the household. A man's role was to protect his wife and earn enough money to support the family. A woman was expected to be obedient to her husband. The Codex Nuttall tells us wives were told:

Miniature mask representing the god Ixtiton. He brought children peaceful sleep.

'Obey your husband cheerfully. Do not scorn him for you will offend the goddess Xochiquetzal.'

Source – Codex Nuttall, 16th century

Growing Up Aztec Glossary

astronomy	*Study of stars and planets*		*is worthless*
fertility	*Able to have babies*	**umbilical cord**	*Cord that gives baby*
midwives	*Women who deliver babies*		*food and oxygen when*
obedient	*Do what you are told*		*it is in the womb*
robust	*Strong and healthy*	**Xochiquetzal**	*Goddess of beauty,*
scorn	*Feeling that something*		*love and housekeeping*

See also: Language and Writing 10–11; Food and Drink 16–17; Aztec Society 22–23; Wars and Warfare 26–27

CASE STUDY

This illustration from the Florentine Codex of Aztec Life shows men crafting stone, c.1570.

Duties of Man

The Aztecs had firm ideas about what made a good citizen. Poems reveal their **EXPECTATIONS** of life:

'Act! Cut wood, work the land, plant cactus, sow maguey; you shall have drink, food, clothing. With this you will stand straight, With this you shall live. For this you shall be spoken of, praised; in this manner you will show yourself to your parents and relatives. Someday you shall tie yourself to a skirt and blouse. What will she drink? What will she eat? You are the support, the remedy; you are the eagle, the tiger. Do not throw yourself upon women ... Hold back with your heart until you are a grown man, strong and robust.'

Source – Miguel León-Portilla, Aztec Thought and Culture, 16th century

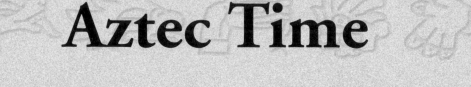

The Aztecs believed there had been four worlds before this one and that they were living in the 'fifth sun' under Tonatiuh the sun god. They also believed that, any day, the world they lived in could be DESTROYED by fiery rain and that people would be turned into dogs, turkeys and butterflies. The Aztecs used two CALENDARS – the solar calendar (365 days) and the religious calendar (260 days). Using both calendars together meant that the same date only recurred once every 52 years.

THE STONE OF THE SUN

The Stone of the Sun is a large circular stone slab that was found in Tenochtitlan in 1760. It is carved with intricate designs which would once have been brightly coloured – as in the reproduction below. It shows the five periods (or 'suns') of CREATION in Aztec mythology. The Stone of the Sun shows us the Aztec HISTORY of their universe.

In the centre is the face of the Sun God Tonatiuh. He has a flint knife for a tongue. This part of the Stone is supposed to show the fifth world.

Tonatiuh is surrounded by four boxes, containing glyphs which show the date of the destruction of the previous four world periods. These worlds were 4-Jaguar (destroyed by jaguars); 4-Wind (destroyed by hurricanes); 4-Rain (destroyed by fire); and 4-Water (destroyed by floods).

These signs show the 20 named days in each month. They are also used for naming years.

The rim features two fire serpents. They represent the creation of the fifth world.

Words to use in your project

ceremony (special occasion)
destruction (damage that cannot be repaired)

doom (terrible fate)
fate (events that cannot be controlled)

prophecy (predicting the future)
rebirth (to start again, or revive)

THE RELIGIOUS CALENDAR

This image from the Codex Borbonicus shows the male and female creator gods discussing the organisation of time. The male god Ometecuhtli is on the right, and the female god Omecihuatl is on the left.

Priests kept notes of the 260-day religious calendar ('tonalpohualli') in **SACRED** books known as 'tonalamatl'. The most famous example of a tonalamatl is the Codex Borbonicus. The pages of this codex show the 13 Lords of the day and nine Lords of the night. These were arranged to show their power over individual hours and days, and also over important 13-day weeks. The tonalamatl were considered to have magical properties, and were used by priests to make predictions.

Aztec Time Glossary

extinguished	Finished, put an end to	**solar**	Related to the sun
intricate	Very detailed	**tonalamatl**	Sacred Aztec book
sacrifice	Where a human being dies for a religious reason as an offering to the gods	**tonalpohualli**	The Aztec religious calendar or day count of 20 'weeks' of 13 days each

See also: Language and Writing 10–11; Religion and Sacrifice 24–25; The End of the Aztecs 30–31

CASE STUDY

The New Fire Ceremony

When a cycle of 52 years approached an end, the Aztecs believed the **FUTURE** of the world was uncertain. Five days before the end of the cycle, Aztecs extinguished all fires, threw away all their belongings and cleaned their homes in preparation for the end of the world. On the night before the end of the cycle, priests marched to the Hill of the Star outside Tenochtitlan. A victim was sacrificed by lighting a fire in his chest and burning his heart. Runners lit torches from the fire and took the flames to their own communities. The next day, people put on new clothes, bought new things for their homes and whitewashed their houses. Humankind was saved!

This scene from the Codex Borbonicus shows the New Fire Ceremony.

Aztec Society

Aztec behaviour was very regimented. The emperor was at the top of society, with NOBLES beneath him. Beneath the nobles were the COMMONERS, and at the bottom of society were the SLAVES. People had to follow strict social codes. Anyone who broke them faced harsh punishments. Thieves were sold as slaves or put to death.

NOBLES AND COMMONERS

Nobles ran the economic, religious and political elements of daily life.

The nobles paid no taxes, and were given a house and farmland, which would provide their income. The emperor controlled the nobles. It was possible for a noble to rise to the position of emperor. The historian Alonso de Zorita recorded how this could happen:

'When there were no brothers to choose from ... the council elected the most capable relative of the deceased ruler; and if there was none, they chose another noble, but they never elected a ... common man.'

Commoners ('macehualtin') were organised into clans known as 'calpulli' which were divided into units of 20 families and arranged in groups of 100 households. Each calpulli had its own school and temple, and was controlled by a leader elected for life. The benefits of belonging to a calpulli were not shared by the free but landless PEASANTS known as 'mayeques'.

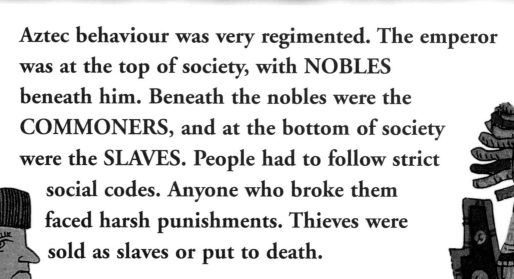

The Codex Mendoza shows Aztec nobles wearing their distinctive cloaks, wearing jewellery and seated on reed thrones.

Source – Alonso de Zorita, 16th century

Words to use in your project

behaviour (*way somebody acts*)
expedition (*journey with a set purpose*)

emancipated (*to be freed*)
finery (*jewellery*)
hierarchy (*ranking system*)

punishment (*inflicting a penalty on somebody*)
tribute (*tax*)

SLAVERY

This image from the Codex Vaticanus shows Chalchiuhtlicue, goddess of lakes and rivers, being attended by slaves.

Nobody was born into slavery but you could become one for reasons ranging from not paying taxes to losing bets. **CRIMINALS** became the slaves of the person they had committed the crime against, while it was also possible to sell yourself or your children into slavery. In Aztec society, slaves were often given as tribute by conquered tribes. *The Book of the Gods and Rites* shows men and women traders buying and selling slaves at market. The slaves are shown wearing wooden collars around their necks which prevented them escaping. It was, however, possible for a slave to purchase his freedom at any time. Woman slaves could also gain their freedom by marrying their owner.

Source – Diego Durán, *The Book of the Gods and Rites and the Ancient Calendar*, 16th century

Aztec Society Glossary

acquired — Gained something

calpulli — (singular: calpolli) – A neighbourhood where a profession or clan lived

clan — A group connected by family/blood ties

economy — The way people make their living – money matters

like trade and finance

obsidian — Dark glass-like rock

pochteca — Nahuatl word for 'merchant'

regimented — Strictly structured

social codes — The way people in a society are expected to behave

See also: Language and Writing 10–11; Aztec Homes 12–13; Aztec Rulers 14–15; Growing Up Aztec 18–19

CASE STUDY

This stone model, found in the Great Temple, shows a merchant carrying goods using a headstrap.

Traders

MERCHANTS known as 'pochteca' belonged to a special class in Aztec society. In the Florentine Codex, the Spanish priest Sahagún shows three pictures of pochteca, seated before the emperor, travelling across Mexico, and trading jewellery and obsidian blades. Merchants were not allowed to display their wealth in public, so returned to the capital at night, recorded by Sahagún:

*'Not by day but by night they swiftly entered by boat ...
And when he had quickly come to unload what he had acquired, then swiftly he took away his boat. When it dawned, nothing remained.'*

Source – Florentine Codex, Bernardino de Sahagún, 1580

Religion and Sacrifice

The Aztecs worshipped more than 200 GODS. Every town, tribe, craft and social class had its own god, and there were gods of creation, of rain and the different crops, and of war and death. The Aztecs were constantly trying to repay the gods by acts of SACRIFICE, in the hope that they might look kindly upon them.

AZTEC GODS

The Aztecs had gods of wind, fire, and water; of childbirth, disease, and misfortune; as well as of the sun, moon and stars.

The two most important gods in Aztec religion were the sun god Huitzilopochtli, and the rain god Tlaloc. Each was worshipped in his own shrine on the summit of the Great **TEMPLE**. The Aztecs also believed that the god Quetzalcoatl created man:

'After the gods had assembled at Teotihuacan, and the sun had been created, they asked themselves who would inhabit the earth ... Quetzalcoatl approached Mictlantecuhtli and Mictlancihuatl (Lord and Lady of the region of the dead); at once he spoke to them: "I come in search of the precious bones in your possession." And Mictlantecuhtli asked of him "What shall you do with them, Quetzalcoatl?" Once again Quetzalcoatl said "The gods are anxious that someone should inhabit the earth".'

Huitzilopochtli, god of sun and war, is shown here carrying a leather shield and banner – from the Codex Magliabecchiano.

The Aztecs believed that after death, a warrior who had been sacrificed or killed in battle went to the Eastern **PARADISE**, women who died in childbirth went to the Western paradise, people who had died by accident or disease went to the southern paradise of Tlaloc, and people who died of old age went to Mictlan – the land of Mictlantecuhtli, god of death.

Source – Anonymous Mexican manuscript, 1558

Words to use in your project

bloodthirsty *(desire to kill and harm)*
placate *(to calm or please somebody)*
prayer *(solemn request or thanks given to a god)*
Omnipotent *(all-powerful)*
terrify *(to make someone feel very scared)*

THE GREAT TEMPLE

The skull altar, or Tzompantli, from the Great Temple.

The Aztecs built a double-temple called the Templo Mayor (the Great Temple) dedicated to the war god Huitzilopochtli and the rain god Tlaloc. The main temple courtyard originally covered almost 25 hectares and had 70 different buildings, including a **SKULL RACK** for 136,000 human skulls, a ritual ball-court, a stone for gladiator sacrifices, a temple to the god Xipe Totec (for more sacrifices), a temple to the god Quetzalcoatl, warriors' houses and the priests' school. The size of the Great Temple impressed everybody who saw it, including Hernán Cortés:

'There are, in all districts of this great city, many temples or houses for their idols. Amongst these temples there is one, the principal one, whose great size and magnificence no human tongue can describe …There are priests … who live there permanantly … dress in black and never comb their hair.'

Religion and Sacrifice Glossary

awash	Flooded with liquid	**Quetzalcoatl**	The priest god, and god of learning and wind
ball court	The court for the Aztec religious ball game tlachtli	**skull rack**	A cage/box to hold the skulls of sacrificed human beings
misfortune	Bad luck		
mosaic	Picture made by arranging small pieces of tile or glass	**social class**	A person's rank in society

See also: Origin of the Aztecs 4–5; Rise of an Empire 6–7; Aztec Time 20–21; Wars and Warfare 26–27

CASE STUDY

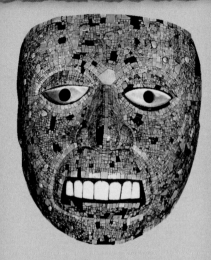

Turquoise mosaic mask to the god Quetzalcoatl, worn for sacrifice.

Sacrifice at the Great Temple

The Aztecs used temples and shrines for worshipping gods through acts of **RITUAL DEATH**. A typical sacrifice took place at the top of the Templo Mayor. The victim was stretched out on the sacrificial stone, the chest cut open, the heart ripped out and the body thrown down the steps.

'The usual method of sacrifice was to open the victim's chest, pull out his heart while he was still half-alive, and then knock down the man, rolling him down the temple steps which were awash with blood … Six sacrificers came in … four to hold the victim's feet and hands, another for the throat, and one to cut the chest and extract the victim's heart. They were called chachalmua, which in our language is the same thing as a minister of sacred things.'

Source – José de Acosta, *Natural and Moral History of the Indies*, 1590

25

Wars and Warfare

The Aztecs waged war in a different way from modern societies. Wars were carried out to make enemies pay tribute, and to capture PRISONERS for sacrifice to the gods. Victory was gathering wealth in tribute from defeated enemies, not slaughtering thousands of people. The Aztecs did not have a standing army, but from a young age, men were trained for battle. Boys were taught at school how to grow up to be WARRIORS, and they were judged according to the number of prisoners they had captured in battle.

ELITE SOCIETIES

Archaeologists digging at the Great Temple site in Mexico City found two life-size, pottery statues guarding the entry to the main room.

Each one represented a man dressed in the feathers of a giant eagle, with his head peering out of the bird's open beak. They matched illustrations from the codices of the **EAGLE KNIGHTS** – members of one of the two great military societies that élite Aztec soldiers were invited to join. A temple has also been found at Malinalco, just outside Mexico City, dedicated to the two élite Aztec warrior societies of the Jaguar and the Eagle. European soldiers were amazed by the bravery of these Aztec soldiers:

'And I do not know how I can write this so calmly, because some three or four soldiers who were in Italy, who were there with us, swore many times to God, that they had never seen such ferocious fighting, like those that were found between Christians and against the artillery of the King of France, or of the Great Turk; nor men like those Indians, with so much courage in closing their ranks, and they said many other things, and the reasons they gave for them, as they would later see.'

An Eagle Warrior statue recovered from the Great Temple.

Source – Bernal Díaz de Castillo, The Conquest of New Spain, 16th century

WEAPONS

Aztec body armour was made out of strengthened cotton, and was more for show than genuine protection from injury on the battlefield. Warriors carried shields decorated with feather, mosaic or gold and turquoise inlay, and their weapons were javelins, bows, slings, and swords. **JAVELINS** were launched with spear-throwers (atlatl) to enable warriors to give greater distance to the weapon. Aztec swords (maquahuitl) were made of wood with edges of obsidian blades that would have been sharp enough to slice straight through an enemy's body.

Feathered shield, made of gold and feathers, showing coyote or ahuitzol, a mythical water creature (above), and Aztec spear thrower (below).

Wars and Warfare Glossary

atlatl	Device that helps throw javelins further than normal	maquahuitl	A sword-club, with an obsidian cutting-edge
elite	People seen as the best	standing	
hostilities	Fighting	army	Permanent army
inlay	Different materials added to a surface	tribute	Payment made to more powerful state, like a tax

CASE STUDY

An Aztec warrior shown capturing an enemy soldier by grasping his hair, from the Codex Mendoza.

War of Flowers

The War of Flowers (xochiyaoyotl) were created to capture prisoners for sacrifice to the gods, rather than for conquest. It was a special type of warfare. **PRIESTS** observed these battles and once they decided that enough prisoners had been taken, hostilities ended. The name refers to the costumes of warriors, and how they fell in battle like a shower of blossoms. The brother of Moctezuma I urged young men to join in these wars:

'Huitzilopochtli, the young warrior who acts above! He follows my path. Not in vain did I dress myself in yellow plumes, for I am he who has caused the sun to rise.'

Source – Miguel León-Portilla, Aztec Thought and Culture, 16th century

See also: Rise of an Empire 6–7; Aztec Rulers 14–15; Growing Up Aztec 18–19; Religion and Sacrifice 24–25

Leisure

Having fun was very important to the Aztecs. Hunting and gambling were very popular, as were GAMES such as 'tlachtli' and 'patolli'. Many of these games had religious meanings, and were taken very seriously, sometimes ending in death or destitution for the loser. MUSIC, poetry and dance were also important. These skills were used in the many religious festivals that occurred in the Aztec year.

GAMES

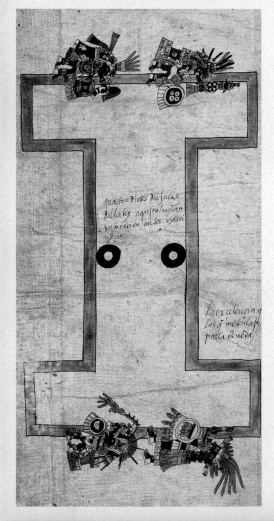

Tlachtli was a ball game for nobles.

It was played on a large court shaped like a letter 'I'. The aim was to put the ball through one of two vertical hoops on the side of the court using just their knees and hips. The court was supposed to represent the world, and the ball the sun or moon. Bets were often placed on the game. Emperor Axayacatl bet the Great Market place in a game against the lord of Xochimilco. Axayacatl did not accept defeat graciously:

'While they saluted him and made him presents, they threw a garland of flowers about his neck with a thong hidden in it, and so killed him.'

Patolli was a **GAMBLING** game played with dice. Like tlachtli, the game had a religious meaning. The board had 52 squares, the same number of years in the dual calendar, and the Aztecs believed that the god Macuilxochitl watched over every game.

This illustration of a ball game is from the Codex Borbonicus, a 16th-century Aztec post-conquest manuscript.

Words to use in your project

chants (repeated phrases shouted or sung by a group)	**leisure** (time spent outside work for enjoyment)
destiny (fate)	**retribution** (punishment inflicted as revenge)
	victorious (someone who defeats an enemy at something)

MUSIC, SINGING AND DANCING

This illustration of an Aztec dance comes from a 1579 manuscript, Historia de las Indias by Diego Durán.

The Aztecs loved music, singing and dancing. The main **INSTRUMENTS** in an Aztec band were the drums, which provided the beat, to which the people added their chants. Other instruments included hollow shells, pottery whistles and rattles, so there was not much of a tune to Aztec music, apart from the singing. Music and dance were performed at religious festivals, so they had to be perfect – they were not for fun! If a musician or singer spoiled the song at the court of Moctezuma, he was put to death. Spanish observers were intrigued by Aztec music, but found the **DANCING** offensive:

'Young people took great pride in their ability to dance, sing, and guide the others in the dances ... There was another dance so roguish ... with all its wriggling and grimacing and immodest mimicry ... it is highly improper.'

Source – Diego Durán, Historia de las Indias de Nueva España, 16th century

Leisure Glossary

destitution	Extreme poverty	**philosopher**	A great and clever thinker
garland	Necklace of flowers	**roguish**	Mischievous
mimicry	Imitation of someone or something else	**tlachtli**	A ball-game played by teams on a special court
patolli	A gambling board-game	**vertical**	Straight up and down

See also: Language and Writing 10–11; Aztec Rulers 14–15; Growing Up Aztec 18–19

CASE STUDY

Xochipilli was the Aztec god of flowers, love, dance and poetry.

Aztec Poetry

Art, literature and **POETRY** were an important part of Aztec life. Priests and nobles prided themselves on their skill at these disciplines, while some emperors were also renowned for their poetry. The Aztec word for poetry means 'flowers-and-song'. The concept element 'flowers' recurs throughout their poems, as a symbol of beauty, of life, and of the gods. An Aztec believed that his poems were one way he could live for ever. Aztec poems are full of worry about what would happen after death. This poem from the philosopher Nezahualcoyotl (1403–1473) expresses this concern:

'One day we must go, one night we will descend into the region of mystery. Here, we only come to know ourselves; only in passing are we here on earth ... Would that one lived forever; would that one were not to die.'

Source – Diego Durán, Historia de las Indias de Nueva España, 16th century

The End of the Aztecs

By 1517, SPANIARDS exploring the coast of Mexico were bringing back stories of a fabulous city high up in the mountains. Hernán Cortés persuaded the governor of Cuba to let him make an expedition to find this city. He gathered together a fleet of ships, soldiers, sailors, crossbowmen, and musketeers, and on November 8th, 1519 he and his 'conquistadors' marched into Tenochtitlan to meet Moctezuma II.

SPANISH INVASION

When the Spanish arrived in Mexico, they were greeted with AWE by the Aztecs, who saw the white, bearded beings, dressed in metal armour as gods.

Even the Aztec Emperor, Moctezuma II, was totally **TRUSTING** of the Spanish and gave Cortés a warm welcome.

'Moctezuma, the great and powerful prince of Mexico ... sent five chieftains of the highest ranks to our camp ... to bid us welcome ... When we entered the town (of Tlaxcala) there was no room in the streets or on the roofs, so many men and women having come out with happy faces to see us.'

But soon, the mood changed and Spanish writers tell us that Cortés revealed his intentions:

'On entering the palace, Cortés made his usual salutations, and said to Moctezuma: "If you cry out, or raise any commotion, you will immediately be killed by these captains of mine, whom I have brought for this sole purpose."'

Hernan Cortés meets Indians from a painting on Tlaxcala walls.

Source – Bernal Díaz de Castillo, The Conquest of New Spain, 16th century

FALL OF TENOCHTITLAN

Once they had arrived in Tenochtitlán, Spanish troops stayed in the city. During this time, Spanish forces **MASSACRED** thousands of members of the Aztec nobility, creating uproar. Moctezuma himself was taken hostage. When he tried to calm a restless crowd in the city, he was killed by a stone thrown from the crowd. Eventually the Aztec forces surrounded the palaces where the Spanish were living, and forced them out, resulting in many deaths. Then, in 1521, Cortés returned to Tenochtitlan with 700 Spanish soldiers and 70,000 native troops – including the Tlaxcalan army. He besieged the city until, in August 1521, it surrendered. The Spaniards and their allies entered the city and massacred the people. The last Aztec ruler, Cuauhtemoc, was captured and **HANGED**. The writer Fernando de Alva Ixtlilxochitl records the tragic scene:

'Almost all those Aztec nobility died, the only survivors being a few lords and gentlemen, mostly children or extremely young people.'

Source – Fernando de Alva Ixtlilxochitl, Historia de la Nación Chichemeca, 16th century

The End of the Aztecs Glossary

allies	People who help you fight your enemies	**hostage**	Prisoner
besieged	To surround a place, and force the people inside to surrender	**inconceivable**	Impossible to imagine
		intentions	Plans
		massacred	Murdered many people
conquistadors	Spanish word for conquerors	**musketeer**	A soldier who fought with a musket (an early form of rifle)

See also: Aztec Rulers 14–15; Aztec Society 22–23; Religion and Sacrifice 24–25; Wars and Warfare 26–27

CASE STUDY

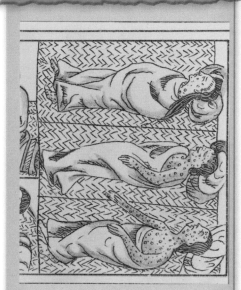

An illustration of Aztec women suffering from smallpox, taken from the Codex Florentine.

Smallpox

Cortés had conquered the Aztec empire. But the man who did the most to destroy it was an unnamed Spanish soldier who came to help Cortés in April 1520 – and who had **SMALLPOX**. The Aztecs had no immunity to this new disease and in the next two years perhaps half a million of them died from it. A tiny germ proved to be a more powerful weapon than all Cortés' guns and horses. Bernal Diaz describes the spread of the disease:

'The disease spread with inconceivable rapidity, and the Indians died by thousands; for not knowing the nature of it they brought it to a fatal issue by throwing themselves into cold water in the heat of the disorder.'

Source – Bernal Díaz de Castillo, The Conquest of New Spain, 16th century

Index

A
alliance/allied 6, 32
astronomy/astrology 11, 18–19
Aztlan 4–5

B
bet(s) 23, 28
boys 18–19, 26
builders/building 7–9, 12, 14, 25

C
calendar(s) 10, 20–21, 28
calpulli 22–23
city(ies) 5, 8–9, 14, 31
civilisation(s) 4–5
codex/codices 10–11, 18, 21
Codex Florentine 11, 13–15, 17, 19, 23, 31
Codex Mendoza 7–8, 10–11, 18–19, 22–23, 26
common(ers) 9, 14–15, 18, 22
conquistadors 30–31
Cortés, Hernán 4, 8–9, 12, 25, 30–31
coronation 15
courtyard 12–13

creation 20
culture 4, 7

D
death 14, 22, 24, 28–29
die 16
drawings 10
Durán, Diego 4, 7–8, 14–16, 29

E
empire 4, 6–7, 11, 14–16, 28, 30, 32
emperor(s) 7, 14–15, 19, 22–23, 28–29, 32

F
farming 16–17
festivals 16–17, 28–29
food 7
future 15, 21

G
games 28–29
girls 18–19
glyphs 10–11
god(s) 7–8, 18, 24, 26, 28–30

H
highland(s) 4–5
history 7, 10

house(s)/household 9, 12–14, 19, 22, 25
Huitzilopochtli 5, 7, 24–25

I
information 11
instruments 29
irrigate/irrigation 13, 17
island(s)/artificial islands 5, 17

K
king(s) 6–7, 9, 11, 14–15, 26, 29

L
lake(s)/Lake Texcoco 4–5, 16–17
language(s) 4, 10
law(s) 11, 14

M
maguey 12, 14, 16, 18–19
maize 16–17
market 8–9, 16, 23, 28
marriage/married 18–19, 23
massacred 31
mat(s) 12, 18
merchants 11, 23
Mexica 4–5, 7, 11
Mexico/Mexico City 4–8, 10, 12–14, 23, 26, 28, 30, 32

Moctezuma, Emperor 14-15, 27, 29–31

N
nobles 12, 14, 18, 22, 28–29, 31

P
palace(s) 13–14, 31
peasant(s) 12, 22
philosopher(s) 11, 29
pictographs 10–11
poetry 28–29
power 6
priest(s) 11, 15, 18, 21, 25, 27, 29
prisoners 26–27
promised land 5

R
religious 11, 20, 22, 28–29
ritual(s)/ritual death 11, 25
ruler(s) 9–10, 14–15, 22, 31

S
sacred 21
sacrifice(d)(s) 21, 24–27
Sahagún, Bernadino 9, 11, 13, 15, 17, 23
school(s) 18, 22, 25–26
scribes 7, 10–11

shield(s) 7, 10, 19, 27
slaves 22–23
smallpox 31
soldier(s) 9, 14, 26, 30–31
song(s) 11, 29
Spain/Spanish/Spaniards 4, 9–11, 18, 30–32
sun(s) 8, 20, 24, 28
symbols 10, 19

T
temple(s)/Great Temple 8, 10–11, 18, 22, 24–26
tribes 5
Tenochtitlan 4–9, 14, 16, 20–21, 30–32
tlatoani 6, 13–15, 22, 32
town(s) 6–7, 13, 17, 24
tribute 7, 16, 26

V
volcanoes 5

W
walls 12
war/warfare 6, 18, 23–24, 26–27
warrior(s) 7, 11, 14, 24–27
water 8–9, 24
weapons 7
writing 10–11

AZTEC TIMELINE

1175
Fall of Toltec civilisation

1200
Arrival of Aztecs in Central Mexico

1250
Aztecs move to Valley of Mexico

1325
Tenochtitlan built

1372
First Aztec Tlatoani appointed

1426
Escalation of conflict between Aztecs and Tepanecs

1428
Aztec Empire established with victory of the Triple Alliance

1519–1521
Spanish Conquest

1520
Last Aztec emperor appointed